TOOLS FOR TEACHERS

- **ATOS:** 0.8
- **GRL:** A
- **WORD COUNT:** 45
- **CURRICULUM CONNECTIONS:** nature, trees

Skills to Teach

- **HIGH-FREQUENCY WORDS:** have
- **CONTENT WORDS:** bark, branches, flowers, fruit, holes, homes, leaves, needles, nests, nuts, roots, seeds, trees, trunks, twigs
- **PUNCTUATION:** periods
- **WORD STUDY:** irregular plural (*leaves*); initial consonant clusters (*branches*, *flowers*, *fruit*, *trees*, *trunks*, *twigs*); long /e/, spelled ee (*needles*, *seeds*, *trees*), ea (*leaves*)
- **TEXT TYPE:** information report

Before Reading Activities

- Read the title and give a simple statement of the main idea.
- Have students "walk" though the book and talk about what they see in the pictures.
- Introduce new vocabulary by having students predict the first letter and locate the word in the text.
- Discuss any unfamiliar concepts that are in the text.

After Reading Activities

Ask children to think of how we use trees; for example, they might answer that we use them for shade or to make paper. Write their responses on the board. Then encourage them to think of other animals that might use trees, such as birds, insects, or small mammals. How do these animals use trees? They might respond that the animals use trees for food or to make their homes. Write their answers on the board as well and discuss.

Tadpole Books are published by Jump!, 5357 Penn Avenue South, Minneapolis, MN 55419, www.jumplibrary.com

Editorial: Hundred Acre Words, LLC **Designer:** Anna Peterson

Photo Credits: Alamy: Kitchin and Hurst, 3; William Leaman, 14. Getty: Panoramic Images, 2. Shutterstock: apiguide, 9; D and D Photo Sudbury, 13; DR Travel Photo and Video, 12; Gerald A. DeBoer, 15; jakkapan, 1; Kenneth Keifer, 8; Martin Fowler, 11; Matauw, 10; Nadezhda Bolotina, 4–5; Peter Kniez, 6; ukmooney, cover; watin, 7.

Library of Congress Cataloging-in-Publication Data
Names: Mayerling, Tim, author.
Title: I see trees / by Tim Mayerling.
Description: Minneapolis, Minnesota: Jump!, Inc., 2017. | Series: Outdoor explorer | Includes index.
Identifiers: LCCN 2017036930 (print) | LCCN 2017039854 (ebook) | ISBN 9781624967238 (ebook) | ISBN 9781620319499 (hardcover: alk. paper) | ISBN 9781620319505 (pbk.)
Subjects: LCSH: Trees—Juvenile literature.
Classification: LCC QK475.8 (ebook) | LCC QK475.8 .M39 2017 (print) | DDC 582.16—dc23
LC record available at https://lccn.loc.gov/2017036930

OUTDOOR EXPLORER

I SEE TREES

by Tim Mayerling

TABLE OF CONTENTS

I SEE TREES

trunk

Trees have trunks.

Trees have bark.

Trees have branches.

Trees have twigs.

Trees have needles.

Trees have leaves.

Trees have flowers.

Trees have fruit.

Trees have nuts.

seed

Trees have seeds.

Trees have roots.

Trees have nests.

Trees have holes.

Trees have homes.

WORDS TO KNOW

bark

flowers

fruit

leaves

needles

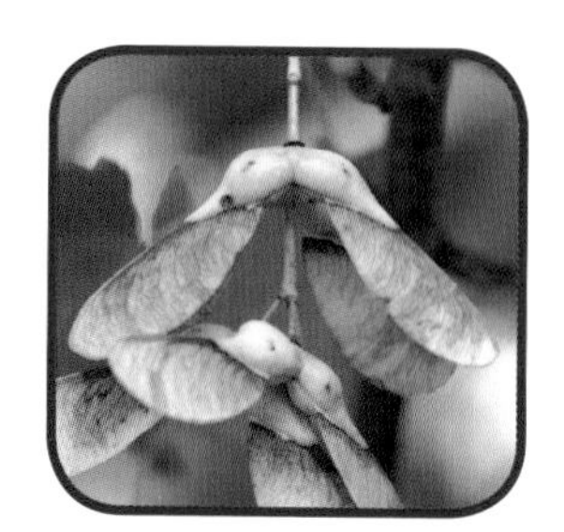
seeds

INDEX